A Declaration
of Legal Faith

Da Capo Press Reprints in

AMERICAN CONSTITUTIONAL AND LEGAL HISTORY

GENERAL EDITOR: LEONARD W. LEVY
Brandeis University

A Declaration of Legal Faith

by

Wiley Rutledge

DA CAPO PRESS • NEW YORK • 1970

A Da Capo Press Reprint Edition

This Da Capo Press edition of *A Declaration of Legal Faith* by
Wiley Rutledge is an unabridged republication of the first edition
published in Lawrence, Kansas, in 1947. It is reprinted by special
arrangement with The University Press of Kansas.

Library of Congress Catalog Card Number 74-114563

SBN 306-71921-5

Published by Da Capo Press
A Division of Plenum Publishing Corporation
227 West 17th Street, New York, N.Y. 10011

Manufactured in the United States of America

A Declaration of Legal Faith

A Declaration
of Legal Faith

by

Wiley Rutledge

University of Kansas Press - Lawrence, Kansas

1947

PRINTED IN THE U.S.A. BY
THE UNIVERSITY OF KANSAS PRESS
LAWRENCE, KANSAS

Prefatory Note

The lectures which comprise the substance of this book, given in Lawrence on December 2-4, 1946, are the first of a series to be delivered periodically at the University of Kansas in honor of Judge Nelson Timothy Stephens, founder of the School of Law at the University. The Judge Stephens Lectureship of the School of Law is supported by an endowment left by his daughter, Miss Kate Stephens, who was a successful author and critic and an alumna of the University. Miss Stephens' father was for many years the presiding judge of the trial court of general jurisdiction in Lawrence, Kansas. Prior to that, he had been a soldier in the Civil War. His belief in the importance of law to society was deeply rooted. In establishing the Lectureship, his daughter expressed the hope that it would "stimulate such independent thought and humane action as distinguished" her father and would make clear, among other truths, the great truth that civilized "life arose as the result of law."

The faculty of the School of Law consider it an especial honor that the busy and distinguished Associate Justice Wiley Rutledge of the United States Supreme Court was willing to inaugurate the Stephens Lectureship; and we wish to express our deep appreciation of his courtesy.

F. J. MOREAU, Dean.

Contents

A Declaration of Legal Faith

A Declaration of Legal Faith

IN establishing these lectures to honor her father's memory, Miss Stephens wished to "stimulate such independent thought and humane action" as characterized his life. To this end she asked that the discourses treat of two large ideas. One is "the essentials of free government," the other that life itself has its origins in law. Her faith rested in a "purposeful striving in evolutionary processes." And she sought to view "discoveries in nature and gains in science" as strengthening in human beings "reverence for the limitless and ordered energy of the Cosmos." Thus in her thinking were joined together the moral law and civil institutions. She conceived that in this nexus lay the prime question of our day.

I am honored to have part in instituting the Stephens lectures, though unequal to the large philosophic task the founder had in mind. She did not survive man's latest and most cosmic struggle, which put in jeopardy the very existence of free government throughout the earth. But if she had lived through it, she could not have stated more clearly the central question of our time, for man and for his future.

It is indeed no new inquiry, whether there may be a "purposeful striving in evolutionary processes." For this is simply one of the nineteenth century's ways of asking the question as old as man himself, namely, whether his universe has moral meaning or gives him only illusion of moral being. Nor is the idea novel that, as one or the other answer is given, it will be reflected inevitably in the character of man's governing institutions.

Variously have men answered the underlying philosophic question, as individuals and as members of society, responding to "the felt necessities" of time and place. Many have been the conflicts between viewpoints exemplified on the one hand by progressing scientific discovery and on the other by established institutions of religion and politics. Almost if not quite as many and as varied have been the eventual reconciliations.

I do not intend to reëxamine this most profound of philosophic inquiries. But two things I wish to say. One is that man cannot escape responding one way or another in the fashioning of his political and legal institutions. The other, that in the end the philosophic question cannot be answered solely by philosophy or by reason or by science. It is a matter of faith. And faith is more felt than thought. From a universe compounded of order and chance, of fate

4

and free will, of past and future, of good and evil, of all the irreconcilables going to make up the vast interacting stuff of life, each for himself must select what is valid and true to live by and to die by. However guided by reason, the choice at the last must be intuitive, must be felt, or it cannot be complete. So also must nations and societies choose and live by a faith. Else they die.

Society in our day does not differ in this respect from others in earlier times. But never before have men and nations been forced to choice and to faith as now. We cannot say whether Miss Stephens today would ask that "discoveries in nature and gains in science" be "viewed in their use and ability to strengthen" men in "reverence for the limitless and ordered energy of the Cosmos." But the question has become preëminent in human affairs. Science and discovery in the physical universe have come to the point where they force us to ask whether the scheme commands reverence or is a vast suicidal delusion. For men everywhere the question of their use is between fear of inescapable self-destruction and hope that man may yet find ways to control his awful power and utilize it for humane living. The issue of our time, in other words, is whether science has become the master of men or men can remain the masters of science. This they can do only through civil institutions founded in moral conceptions. The question therefore takes form whether man today has the capacity to devise and establish those institutions.

It is because I think this question overshadows and comprehends all others that I wish in this first Stephens lecture to declare my own faith. I shall not ask you to accept it, though I hope you may find it not without support in reason and in your own feeling. For underlying it are the intuitions which to me make life worth living, without which the daily round from sleep to sleep would be only illusion of passing from light to shadow. If to them reason adds in some measure its supporting brace, the intuitions cannot be less valid for this.

I believe in law. At the same time I believe in freedom. And I know that each of these things may destroy the other. But I know too that, without both, neither can long endure.

In every man is the aspiration to be master of his fate, unless indeed "bowed by the weight of centuries" he has become

"dead to rapture and despair,
A thing that grieves not and that never
hopes,
Stolid and stunned, a brother to the ox."

6

That fate the soul of man rejects; and, rejecting, proves he is by nature more than clod, as also that nature comprehends the soul. Man himself aspiring refutes his wholly electrical being and thereby the merely mechanical order of his universe.

In every man is also the yearning for the company and approval of his fellows, an instinct which draws him into the group and dictates his acceptance of its mores. Family, clan, tribe, village, and their modern counterparts satisfy this longing, giving the individual their comforts and protections, but exacting a measure of his freedom as the price of social living.

From the necessity for satisfying both of these cravings, the instinct for freedom and the social instinct, arises the never-ending process of accommodating freedom to law and law to freedom. That process is inherent in any community, whether its professed ideological emphasis lies at one or the other extreme of the order-freedom complex or somewhere in between. The soul of man cannot be altogether and forever bound in, a fact by virtue of which with time the most unyielding despotism must come to earth. On it rests the inalienable right of revolution which our fathers exercised in the Declaration of Independence. On the other hand, unbounded freedom cannot be conceded in society

7

to the individual or group constituent. For this would lead only to anarchy. And man's instinct for order and stability, combining with his yearning for fellow approval, rejects the anarchistic principle as completely as his instinct for liberty denies the despotic one.

There results therefore from the conflicting and isolated instincts for freedom and for social living an accommodating instinct, one seeking to reconcile the opposing extremes. This indeed tends to merge the underlying opposites and to become the dominating need of man's living. For by it he secures what is possible to achieve of both his aspirations.

This need and the process of satisfying it give play to another great drive of human yearning, the desire for and the struggle to achieve justice. It is not enough for man's social living that merely some sort of accommodation be made between his desire for freedom and the demand of the community, as also of himself, for law and stability. In enduring society the drive is ever toward securing the right adjustment between man and man and between the individual and society. This is true though what is right may shift as dominant yearnings swing from freedom to order and back again.

Philosophers and kings have wrestled throughout the ages with the problem of justice, seeking the standard by which acceptable accommodation between these emphases may be made. Nor is the end yet. The conception has not been confined in enduring formula. It cannot be so imprisoned. But this does not prove the unreality of the search or indeed of the vast achievements which have been made in the name of justice. It proves only that ideas of justice must grow and change as man lifts himself from his aboriginal state. It proves that justice too is a part of life, of evolution, of man's spiritual growth.

Again my purpose is not to enter upon the philosophical inquiry, but is rather to declare a faith. I know that cynics have held the idea of justice to be a will-o'-the-wisp, a delusion, at best an abstraction to be filled with whatever content authority, observer, or philosopher may seek to inject. I know too that often great strides backward toward the jungle have been taken. Some have come just at moments when it seemed no such reaction could occur, that a level of civilization had been reached where man had put an impassable barrier between himself and the plunge back to depths from which he had risen. I also know that we live in a time when one of those plunges has taken place, perhaps the longest and most devastating in man's life on earth.

But is this cause for discarding the idea of justice, and with it the effort to accommodate freedom and order in right relationships? If so, we might better have thrown in the sponge before we were dragged into the fight. No man without faith that justice can be achieved, without belief that through its application the better accommodation of social and individual interest can be made in our time, could have taken up the sword or the wrench or the plough for the waging of the war. All that we have suffered and achieved in these years of horror is proof that we have believed to the very depths of our being in justice as a reality, that it can be achieved, that it is not a delusion ensnaring mankind in essential falsity.

This is true although conceptions of justice have differed as among ourselves, as between ourselves and our allies, even as between our enemies and ourselves. I deny that all which has been done and suffered is only proof that we sought the selfish end, the baser thing, to keep what we had of material advantage because we had it and other men should not share. Selfishness there was and is in broad measure. But not all that men gave in North Africa, in Italy, at Iwo Jima, in the Bulge, at Stalingrad and Petrograd, in China and elsewhere throughout the earth, was given for selfishness alone, in denial that justice between man and man can be established and more and more perfected. If this was illusion, still it was the stuff of which the most solid hold on life is made. It was the thing for which men put aside all else and in climactic struggle were willing to give and gave their lives. It was faith, which now as yesterday is the evidence of things unseen, the assurance of things as yet unrealized.

In a broad sense, all this applied even to our enemies. The basic difference between them and us did not lie in affirmation and denial that justice exists, can be achieved, is only a will-o'-the-wisp. It was rather in the vast gulf dividing us concerning what is justice and how it is to be attained, what standards and methods shall determine it in our time. One cannot have heard Herr Hitler's screaming tirades, though understanding not a guttural word, without knowing that they rose from a deep, driving sense of injury and injustice.

But his standard was different from ours. It was national and racial, not individual or inclusive of humanity. The mass was select and supreme. Meaning and place were given to men only as they became or were dissolved in its structure. Justice for them became justice for the group, hence by easy transference for the state; and power accordingly became single, authoritarian, totalitarian, absolute.

But from England came a great voice in contrary tradition, dogged in determination to preserve rights of individual men. And another joined from the waters of the Atlantic to declare again old freedoms and to proclaim new ones for our time. Together they massed the sentiments and powers of their peoples and of other peoples to keep law alive not simply for the group but for men as men.

Thus they drew issue, sharp, clear, and total between their peoples' standards of justice and the enemy's. Two things were involved, the right of one nation to impose its will on others regardless of their wishes; and the right of any nation to make its people the minions of the state rather than the state the servant of the people. The conditions of our time had made these one and inseparable. For science and invention had made it no longer possible for a nation and its people attached to either view to hold assurance of continued life in contiguity with nations and peoples devoted to the contrary principle. Hence to death-clash came these ultimate and irreconcilable notions of justice.

In both conceptions law was seen and used not as an end in itself, but as a means for establishing, maintaining, and perfecting the accepted ideal of justice, of right accommodations in social living. The difference was not as to the function of law. It

concerned the ends which law was to serve. It
marked the distinction between long-evolving traditions of social living. They in turn represented opposing emphases upon order and freedom, the sup-
posed good of the whole and the welfare of the free
individual, together with the relation these bear to
each other. The law became the instrument for securing those traditions, the means for their perpetu-
ation.

Who knows to what extent these opposites in
ideas of justice grew out of differences in geographic
location and historic experience? Who can say
whether the British people or ourselves, situated in
the heart of Europe as were the Germans, having
their historical background and outlook, might not
have come to their view? Who knows whether, if
the pressures on the English and on us should become the same and as long continued, they or we
might not come in time to the German view? And
who knows now whether, if we or any other nation
should do so in days to come, the demonstrated arts
of violence would not establish that view where
Hitler failed?

We cannot answer with assurance. But we do
know that the ideas of justice accepted by a people may bring their destruction. We know that
those ideas change with time and circumstance,

shifting from order to freedom and back again, with danger at both ends of the arc. We know too that law follows these changes, seldom creating them except when the lag becomes too great. Then men revolt, throw aside the archaic legal scheme, and bring another into being consonant with the prevailing mood of right accommodation.

At such times, if ever, arises danger that law may go too far in advance of accepted mores. For in them zealots often seize power and mold the legal institution to their own notions of what the revolution has sought to achieve. Their zeal may overshoot the mark. When this occurs the stage is set for inevitable reaction, often violent.

The problem of justice is thus perpetual. It is not and never can be realized in legal institutions as an abstraction. For in this sense, as the ideal of a society perfectly adjusted in right relationships, justice is a matter of religion, of outlook upon the universe as a whole. Those conceptions necessarily will differ. They touch the most sacred things in life. They cannot be imposed by any state or legal system, without destroying the most basic freedoms of all, the freedoms to think and to believe as one's lights and conscience give him direction and compulsion. Because ideals of perfection differ, because no single ideal of total perfection ever can be completely rea-

14

lized, and because any attempt to bring about such perfection in the form of legal institutions would be only to create the worst tyranny of all, abstract justice is not and cannot become a legal institution. But it is not legally irrelevant. It is the source, the reservoir of basic ideas in society of what is right and just. In time a society must and will accept a partial composite, a segment or segments of agreement from the complex of total and differing views, as a commonly or predominantly conceded basis for social action. Taking not the creed, but the standard of conduct it enjoins, or the same standard dictated by a variety of creeds, the community adopts this as the norm of just behavior. Those norms, when so approved, give concrete content to the idea of justice as a legally recognizable institution. They form the raw material of law. From abstract justice, through concrete justice, to justice according to law is the continuous cycle by which the legal institution evolves and must maintain itself, if just social accommodation is to be found in an orderly way.

This cycle necessarily is fluid in changing society, and at paces varying with the rate of change. So, in the sense of a legally relevant standard, justice is and must be fluid. Likewise with the law. Neither can be static, although the pace of change is different. Ideas of justice commonly accepted change before the legal process can or will reflect them. The *status quo*, the principle of social momentum, resists although it cannot finally block, the indicated revision of the law. The "felt necessities" arise from moving life, to convert an earlier accepted ideal crystallized in law into a negation of justice. But here too "the moving finger writes and having writ moves on." Justice therefore cannot be embalmed in the mores of any day or age. Nor can the law. For if this happens the law finds itself at odds with the moral sense of the community, and thus begins to sow the seeds of revolution.

That justice cannot be static does not mean that it is ephemeral. Rather the meaning is that justice is part of life itself, subject to the law of growth without which all is death. In this sense there is confirmation of the idea that the principle of justice is eternal. For it too is alive and must reach new levels and horizons, as man does in all his higher aspirations.

Justice then, in the legally relevant sense, is not abstract, universal, eternally fixed and immutable, perfect and complete, or dead. It is concrete, finite, ever-changing, imperfect and incomplete, alive. And so with the law, which is not an end in itself but simply the means for achieving justice.

16

Not the perfection of our scheme, therefore, but the knowledge that it may be made more perfect, is what makes it worth fighting for. For this reason only the legislator or the judge who can catch the vision of what has come or will come and sense the moment of its common acceptance, from out the realm of abstract justice into the area of realizable application, is worthy to give his people their laws or judgments.

For those tasks he has no Norden bombsights. But he is not without instruments for objective measurement. He has great and concrete traditions to guide him. He has the experience of his fathers. And so far as the circumstances of his time may differ from theirs, calling for different action, he has the prevailing sense of his community to go by. This is a thing not always easy, but neither impossible, to measure. Not his own will or desire, therefore, but his measurement made to the best of his whole ability of the balance between long-accepted tradition and prevailing demand, must determine his course. Thus and only thus may we have a government of the living law and not a government of the personal whims of men or of law archaic and outworn.

I believe therefore in justice. I believe in abstract justice, though I cannot define it. But in any legal

17

sense I believe in it only as the source from which conceptions of concrete and legally relevant justice arise. I believe in concrete justice, in particular justice, and in the possibility of its growth and expansion. I believe in it as the end of legal institutions and in them as the means by which it may be achieved. I believe too in the growth of the law and in this as the only means for making reconciliation between the conflicting forces and conceptions, separately considered, of order and freedom. Only thus may right accommodations in social living and the maintenance of stable, just social relationships be fulfilled.

Law, freedom, and justice—this trinity is the object of my faith. Lacking any one of those components, the resultant scheme could only be anarchy or tyranny, chaos or despotism. In neither is there room for faith. And so I prefer to think of the law, in Miss Stephens' phrase, as "a purposeful striving in evolutionary processes," and of these not as the blind, automatic workings of physical force, but as themselves processes of living which comprehend man's spirit and its growth, together with the possibility of its death.

So we come back to the prime question whether men can devise legal and political institutions to control their physical powers. If I could not believe that man has the moral capacity to hold in restraint the terrible instruments he has forged, there would be little room for faith of any kind. I do believe he has this power. But I am not too confident he may not be diverted from applying it, by less important things, until it is too late. Notwithstanding doubt, here too one must hold fast to hope. So I come to the last article of my declaration.

I believe that law is universal, if not in the sense that chaos cannot override it, then in the necessity for it now or soon to have universal application, unless justice under law is to perish from the earth. Today the world faces this choice. Men have the power to make it. But they cannot long delay. For now truly more than ever "once to every man and nation comes the moment to decide"; and there is danger we may neglect "the choice momentous till the judgment hath passed by." There still is time; and progress there has been, albeit slow. Again we cannot surrender faith and hope. For without them there can be no striving for or, thus, attainment of the goal.

I have given you my faith in the principle of law and its universality. This has precluded considering specific procedures and methods. Modes of application may make or break a principle for survival in legal as in other social institutions. Men who would create such a system, more especially one to fit a new level of legal action, must work with this in mind and with conditions as they find them. These too must be taken into account in whatever changes they would make.

Just 160 years ago our fathers faced a problem much like the one bearing in upon the world today. They solved it, creating a more perfect union. In spite of many imperfections their solution has brought the nation in freedom and a high measure of security through the world's most turbulent century and a half. They did not destroy all of the framework of government within which the people then lived. They could not have done so. But they abolished the Confederation. They launched a nation in its place. They did so by applying the federal principle to the states then existing. Thus they created the power essential for their time and later. Who can say that thereby they destroyed freedom? Rather they preserved it.

That principle, of federal union, with power adequate for the common need, but safeguarded in the interest of freedom by division between nation and state as well as among departments, gave the only feasible way for achieving the necessary accommodation of their time. It may be that the same principle also will afford the only feasible method today for achieving the same end on broader scale, inclusive of the world. Because I believe the federal principle may be the most practical method for doing this; because too I think it contains the fairest possibility for creating the necessary power and preventing its abuse, I have felt it worth while for us to consider, in the further discussions, an illuminating chapter in federal democratic living.

The Commerce Clause:
A Chapter in Democratic
Living

I

The Pendulums of Power and the Arcs Traversed

IF any liberties may be held more basic than others, they are the great and indispensable democratic freedoms secured by the First Amendment.[1] But it was not to assure them that the Constitution was framed and adopted. Only later were they added, by popular demand. It was rather to secure freedom of trade, to break down the barriers to its free flow, that the Annapolis Convention was called, only to adjourn with a view to Philadelphia. Thus the generating source of the Constitution lay in the rising volume of restraints upon commerce which the Confederation could not check. These were the proximate cause of our national existence down to today.

As evils are wont to do, they dictated the character and scope of their own remedy. This lay specifically in the commerce clause. No prohibition of trade barriers as among the states could have been

---

[1]Thomas v. Collins, 323 U.S. 516, 530; Prince v. Massachusetts, 321 U. S. 158, 164; Cantwell v. Connecticut, 310 U. S. 296; Schneider v. State, 308 U. S. 147; Board of Education v. Barnette, 319 U. S. 624.

effective of its own force or by trade agreements. It had become apparent that such treaties were too difficult to negotiate and the process of securing them was too complex for this method to give the needed relief. Power adequate to make and enforce the prohibition was required. Hence, the necessity for creating an entirely new scheme of government.

The men of Annapolis and Philadelphia were not cowards. Nor were they above a little statesmanly deception in a good cause. They had not been taught that open covenants always should be openly arrived at. So they kept the arriving stage secret. At the beginning they also dissembled a bit in their purpose. Not only were they men of strategy and of vision. They faced the hard facts squarely, a virtue often rejected by ourselves of late. The founders were not wishful thinkers, seeing nasty facts and disregarding them. They rather accepted the conclusion dictated by the facts in the most important matters. So by a stroke as bold as it proved successful, they founded a nation, although they had set out only to find a way to reduce trade restrictions. So also they solved the particular problem causative of their historic action, by introducing the commerce clause in the new structure of power.

The particular solution has been highly successful. Without its results it may well be doubted whether any of the remaining creation could long have survived. For it became the foundation of a prosperity which could not have surmounted the outlawed restrictions. In time it created a continental area of free trade. No other continent save Australia is crossed by as few as two tariff barriers. And no other area, save that of Soviet Russia, embraces so many square miles and people whose trade is not blocked or impeded by such restraints. On this fact as much as any other we may safely say rests the vast economic development and present industrial power of the nation. To it may be credited largely the fact we are an independent and democratic country today. For, together with the will and the strength of our people, it was the basis for victory in the war just closed. The fathers builded better than they knew. One can only speculate what fraction of our industrial might could have been developed if they had failed in solving this crucial problem of their time. One can be almost certain the fraction would not have been equal to this latest test.

Effective as was the commerce clause solution, it nevertheless has not been a simple one for execution. It has become the source of continuing and intricate adjustments for the states, the Congress, the courts, and the people. Deceptively simple in wording, in its application and administration the clause has engendered and become entangled with almost every conceivable complexity to be found in a federal structure, which is itself made complex by the division of power between nation and states and also by distribution of powers at both levels among the three great branches of government.

This experience accordingly has demonstrated the inherent difficulties of administering a federal system at the same time that it has shown how successfully such a system can meet the greatest necessities of large masses of people inhabiting a vast area under varied conditions. Because of this, and its significance for the world need of today, I have thought that in the time remaining we may well consider this chapter from experience in federal democratic living.

The order would be too large, to undertake in two lectures either a survey or a technical discussion of that experience. Both time and the dubious propriety of such an effort by one in my place forbid it. For the relevant present purpose no more is needed than sketching the experience broadly.

Twelve words the founders used: "The Congress shall have Power . . . [3] To regulate Commerce . . . among the several States . . . ."—Art. I, § 8, Constitution.[2]

Simple, those dozen words. They do not in terms forbid the states to act. But by negative implication they stripped the states of ability to lay tariffs or otherwise raise barriers against trade crossing state lines. Nothing was said about judges. But those twelve words have been a headache for judges ever since they were written. The simplicity of wording covers a large intricacy of action.

Congress is given the power to regulate commerce. But what is regulation? Is it prohibition? Is it taxation? And what is commerce? Does it include transportation? If so, only for hire or noncommercial movements also? How about transactions, sales, purchases, correspondence, communications, the making of contracts, conducting a general course of trade, the flight of migratory birds? Does commerce encompass manufacturing, mining, farming, and labor relations involved in those pursuits as well as in transportation and other activities? All

---

[2] They gave the same authority with reference to "Commerce with foreign Nations . . . and with the Indian Tribes." Time has largely taken care of the Indians. Foreign commerce, though closely related, was a distinct matter, in some respects has had a very different history, e.g., in the extent and frequency with which the federal power was exercised as well as the comparative infrequency of attempts by the states to regulate foreign commerce during the first hundred years, and is put to one side both for these reasons and because of limitations of time.

these questions and many others have arisen to require determination of what is commerce. Again, what is interstate? Does such commerce include local activities not touching or crossing state lines, which however "affect" or influence the course of the commerce that does, of whatever nature that may be?

And what is the nature of Congress' power? Is it exclusive or only paramount? This question becomes important when a state has taken some action conceived to be possibly within the scope of the authority given Congress. For then the exclusive or possibly concurrent nature of the power, as relating to Congress alone or both to Congress and the states, comes in question. And this is further refined by the questions whether Congress in fact has acted and, if so, consistently or inconsistently with what the state has done; or, on the contrary, if it has taken no action affirmatively, whether this makes a difference. Still further, can Congress authorize the states to do what otherwise is or may be forbidden?

All this is complicated further by the query, who is to decide these various questions, Congress alone or judges, and in either event finally or subject to possible revision by the other branch?

Of such variety and complexity are the questions those twelve deceivingly simple words have spawned.

In view of their variety and volume, it is interesting that merely the adoption of the clause sufficed substantially to achieve its primary object, for the first century of the nation's life, without the necessity for invoking the active use of Congress' power.[3] Not until roughly the last decade of the nineteenth century, when the Sherman Act and the Interstate Commerce Acts became effective, was there need for more than casual regulation. Then began, slowly at first, the active regulation of business by Congress pursuant to the power given. This was accelerated rapidly first about the time of World War I, then with the New Deal, finally with World War II. Thus was reflected in our laws the change, slow at first, then suddenly speeded up, from a rural, horse-powered economy, with largely water-borne commerce, to the urban, mechanical, mass-production system of today, moving goods in a variety of forms of transport.

But all during the first century, while Congress was inactive and partly for that reason, the states were very active. In the then prevailing conditions

---

[3]See Pennsylvania v. Wheeling and Belmont Bridge Co., 13 How. 518, and compare Pennsylvania v. Wheeling and Belmont Bridge Co., 18 How. 421, and The Clinton Bridge, 10 Wall. 454.

31

of life they were, appropriately, the primary and on the whole effective agencies for regulating business activity. All commerce, including that which is interstate, takes place within their borders, requires legal protection and policing in the interest both of the commerce itself and of the public. The only difference between local and interstate commerce in these respects is that the latter transpires also, in some phase, within the borders of another state or, under the "affectation" doctrine, is substantially influenced by events there.

Necessarily, therefore, while Congress was so long inactive and the states were the primary agencies for regulating business, their regulations frequently impinged upon the trade and commerce which was interstate. Often they were designed to do this. And from this fact flowed a constant stream of cases into the courts attacking the validity of the regulation or its incidence. The commerce clause consequently became the basis for questioning of state action by private individuals in voluminous litigation, grounded upon the scope and character of the prohibition on what the states could do. Largely in this negative approach and perspective was the clause given meaning and application.

From *Gibbons* v. *Ogden*, 9 Wheat. 1, to now this process has gone on, the litigation proceeding in the view, now axiomatic,[4] that although the power to regulate was given to Congress, it is the business of the courts to see that the states do not put their noses in Congress' business, however able Congress might be to take care of that business on its own account. Thus early was the judicial finger stuck in the commerce clause pie and there it has since remained. But it has not remained always inserted in the same places. On occasion it has been shifted to a more comfortable spot.[5]

Because in its federal setting it deals with problems relating to both poles of power, the commerce clause is a uniquely federal instrument. More than any other provision it has had to do with clashes of federal and state power, the lines of their division and their reconciliation in the federal plan. It is, so to speak, a two-edged sword, cutting both ways. One edge is the positive affirmation of national, that is, congressional power. The other, not so smooth or keen, cuts down state power by implied or inferential negation. The process of applying the clause therefore necessitates making accommodation between those competing powers and the interests affected by them.

---

[4] Compare note 7 and text, *infra*; also Part II, note 7 and text, *infra*.
[5] See the cases cited in note 3. Cf. Ribble, State and National Power over Commerce (1937); and discussion, Part II, *infra*, at notes 23, 24.

This is where the courts have come in. Neither power affected, national or state, is without limits. Each is to some extent a restriction on the other.[6] As has been shown, the deceptively simple terms of the commerce clause but broadly indicate the outer boundary of the granted federal power, its general nature, and the area for exclusion or subordination of state power. Moreover, except by possible inference from granting the regulatory power to Congress, there is no hint what agency shall define those limits. Only by virtue of the clause's context with other constitutional provisions and through inferential reference to them, is there suggestion of judicial intervention in these or other respects.

When these questions of accommodation began to come forward a great judge headed the federal judiciary, one with the vision of a nation still forming, still to be perfected and firmly established. More than any other man who did not share in the

---

[6] This does not mean that state power is a limitation upon federal power within the federal sphere. Cf. Prudential Insurance Co. v. Benjamin, 328 U. S. 408, 423. It does mean that, wherever the farthest boundary of the power of Congress may go, that line provides a limit induced by the incidence of state power at that point. Since, however, the states may in some respects regulate interstate commerce, the ultimate boundary of Congress' power in its broadest reaches is not a limit to state power in the sense of total prohibition; it is one only in the sense that Congress can override state action. The areas marking off the broadest bounds of the two powers are not mutually exclusive, nor are they conterminous. They simply overlap, like intersecting circles.

34

work at Philadelphia, save possibly Jefferson, he gave the national institution form and strength. His ideas of federal supremacy, within the broadly granted spheres of action, including with others the judicial power, made him a true architect of the nation's structure. To Marshall's presence on the bench, therefore, when the questions of defining and accommodating commerce powers and the fields of their operation began to arise, must be attributed in no little part the fact that the accommodating function has become so largely judicial. In some particulars his work has gone overboard with time, as it has also in other fields.[7] But those indentations have not affected the magnitude or the strength of his greatest achievement, which lay in the establishment of the federal power, legislative and judicial, as supreme in areas broadly adequate for the nation's future. His work is proof that the business of inter-

---

[7] Thus his ideas of tax immunity, as relating to state and national functions and the subjection of each to taxation by the other, have been greatly modified in their application. See M'Culloch v. Maryland, 4 Wheat. 316, and compare, e.g., the "legal incidence" rule of cases such as James v. Dravo Contracting Co., 302 U. S. 134; Alabama v. King & Boozer, 314 U. S. 1. "The power to tax is the power to destroy" has been qualified by "not while this Court sits." Marshall's genius lay partly in his ability to use broad absolutes, when dealing with the distribution of powers, appropriate if not also necessary in his time, for achieving his great judicial objective, namely, to establish firmly the federal power, including the judicial power, within broad areas appropriate and in his view essential for national action.

preting and applying what others have done can be highly creative.

Gibbons v. *Ogden* will stand for the life of the federal system as a landmark in commerce clause law, as it will also in the law of federal supremacy and of the place of judicial power in the scheme. It dealt with the elementary questions, what is "commerce," what is "regulation," what is the nature or character of the power of Congress in reference to the asserted power of the state to act in the same field?

Those questions are not altogether independent. There is interplay among them. And there is ambiguity in all. We do not yet know how to define commerce with broadly inclusive words of precision.[8] We only know how to chip out the definition bit by bit. But Marshall gave as nearly an enduring and comprehensive formula as has been devised.[9] He undertook also to determine the "nature" of the power to regulate. In his view it was "exclusive,"

---

[8] See Ribble, State and National Power over Commerce (1937) c. VII.

[9] "Commerce, undoubtedly, is traffic, but it is something more: it is intercourse. It describes the commercial intercourse between nations, and parts of nations, in all its branches, and is regulated by prescribing rules for carrying on that intercourse." Gibbons v. Ogden, 9 Wheat. 1, 189-190. Compare the statement of Oakley, counsel for the respondent, that "the correct definition of commerce is, the transportation and sale of commodities." Gibbons v. Ogden, *supra*, at 76.

not tolerant of intrusion by state authority although Congress had taken no affirmative action.[10]

Here the work was not so lasting. For in this phase Marshall used the case, and the decision, as a vehicle for buttressing his main tenet of federal supremacy.[11] In this he succeeded. But when, in doing so, he made the bare unexercised power of Congress "exclusive" and gave it the broad scope for operation comprehended by his definition of commerce his ruling was due for trouble.[12] Had it stood unmodified the effect on state power would have been devastating, in relation to matters vitally affecting state interests arising out of interstate commerce done within the state's borders.

Cooley v. Board of Wardens, 12 How. 299, was to prevent this. By its ruling the federal power retained its exclusive character, whether or not Congress had acted, in areas requiring national uniformity. But it lost that quality in matters regarded as being of primarily local importance so that uniformity was not thought to be required. The states could

---

[10] See Ribble, c. II; Frankfurter, The Commerce Clause (1937) c. I; IV Beveridge, The Life of John Marshall (1919) c. VIII. Marshall could have held the state monopoly unconstitutional by relying solely on the ground that Congress had acted by licensing the coastwise trade. The discussion of the power of the states in the absence of affirmative action by Congress was dictum. See Frankfurter, *supra*, at 15-17, 23.

[11] See Frankfurter, 17-18; Ribble, 21-29.

[12] Cf. notes 7 and 10.

touch those things, though Congress could override
them. And thus a new line was drawn for judicial
administration which has lasted until now, not always however with the most happy results.[13]

All this is a well-known story and well told in
greater detail by others.[14] We need not and cannot
repeat or extend the particulars here. But the story
tells of the beginnings of great trends in accommodation of powers. And with these we are concerned.
The questions, what is commerce, what is regulation, and of their interplay, have concerned the
larger generalizations, and therefore the larger am-
biguities, of the clause's wording. They have affected both arcs of power and the swinging of both
pendulums, national and state. In considering these,
it will be helpful to go back to the language of the
clause and its possible implications.

We turn first to the National Affirmation—"The
Congress shall have Power . . . to regulate Commerce . . . among the several States. . . ." In this, as

---

[13] Compare the judicial difficulties leading to the enactment of the
Longshoremen's and Harbor Workers' Compensation Act, 33 U. S. C.
§901 et seq. See Southern Pacific Co. v. Jensen, 244 U. S. 205; Knicker-
bocker Ice Co. v. Stewart, 253 U. S. 149; Washington v. Dawson & Co.,
264 U. S. 219. See also Parker v. Motor Boat Sales, 314 U. S. 244; Swan-
son v. Marra Bros., 328 U. S. 1.

[14] See, e.g., Frankfurter, The Commerce Clause (1937); Ribble,
State and National Power over Commerce (1937); Gavit, the Commerce Clause (1932); Dowling, Interstate Commerce and State Power
(1940) 27 Va. L. Rev. 1.

compared with the negative implications operative upon the states, the solutions have been relatively easy. There has been concern with what is commerce, not so much with what is regulation. Some trouble has been found, in rare instances, with whether the finding of what is commerce, or what is within reach of the commerce power, is to be made by Congress or by the courts.[15] But this problem has not arisen frequently and when thrown up has been sidetracked, though not too skillfully.[16] The Court here, as in other instances, has been hesitant about declaring an Act of Congress invalid, in a matter concerning which its judgment is entitled to so much weight and deference. But largely the task has been done judicially, of defining the reach of the federal legislative arm.

At first transportation was brought in. Then trade. Later all the things we have mentioned, except possibly the flight of migratory birds,[17] and many others. Down to the present century no Act of Congress was invalidated because of the nature of the subject matter or character of the activity, pro-

---

[15] See Pennsylvania v. Wheeling and Belmont Bridge Co., 13 How. 518, and Pennsylvania v. Wheeling and Belmont Bridge Co., 18 How. 421, and other cases cited in Part II, note 24 *infra*.

[16] Cf. note 15.

[17] Compare State v. Sawyer, 113 Me. 458; State v. McCullagh, 96 Kan. 786, with Missouri v. Holland, 252 U. S. 416.

vided it was shown to involve sufficiently the crossing of state lines.[18] Marshall's definition held water.

But Congress, as we have noted, had legislated little during this time. The judicial pronouncements were made almost exclusively in cases concerning state legislation. In them were some aberrations from the usually broad sweep given the power.[19] And large areas of productive activity were regarded, in the prevailing state of economic development, as not being commerce at all. Ideas of states' rights affected notions of the scope of state and federal power, to make such things as mining, manufacturing, and farming seem local, not national in character and effects, although their products moved interstate. They were done locally and were considered not to come into the realm of commerce until their products were started on interstate journey. The *Shreveport* doctrine had not had birth.[20] The states were the chief, most often the only, active agencies of regulation. Hence, in part, grew up the notion that the powers of the states acted to limit the federal pow-

---

[18]Previously, congressional action had been held unconstitutional because it was thought that the subject regulated related "exclusively to the internal trade of the States," United States v. Dewitt, 9 Wall. 41, 45, or because Congress had attempted to regulate intrastate as well as interstate commerce. Trade-Mark Cases, 100 U. S. 82. See also Stoutenburgh v. Hennick, 129 U. S. 141.
[19] See Paul v. Virginia, 8 Wall. 168.
[20] The Shreveport Rate Cases, 234 U. S. 342.

er, to fix its outer perimeter and thus to define the federal field.[21] Such indeed came to be the prevailing climate of legal thought.

There was however a contrary pull between these ideas and Marshall's broad definition. Accordingly in the cases relating to state action there were conflicting pronouncements. Notwithstanding this, from Marshall to Fuller the congressional power itself remained unimpaired by specific decision. State power was often sustained as being within the rule of permissible local diversity in the field of commerce, less often as being outside its boundary because "commerce" was not involved. With the bulk of regulation being done by the states, and expanding business activity more and more requiring regulation, the result hardly could have been otherwise. For this would have meant no regulation at all in many instances; in others forcing Congress to act, an almost equally abhorrent thing in the prevailing climate.

The first great jolt to Congress' power came with the Knight decision[22] in 1895, outlawing application of the Sherman Act to the sugar trust, on the ground that production rather than commerce was involved. The Act became and remained a dead let-

---

[21] See text immediately preceding note 20.
[22] United States v. E. C. Knight Co., 156 U. S. 1.

ter until it was revived in 1904 in the *Northern Se-curities* case[23] involving transportation. Less than ten years later the *Knight* case, in effect, was over-ruled by the *Standard Oil* and *American Tobacco* cases, later reinforced in the *Coronado* cases.[24]

By this time Congress had become active, and if the strong presumption of the validity of congres-sional legislation[25] was to continue having force, conflict inevitably was to be expected between its application and the pull of prior pronouncements of the breadth of the area open for operation of the states' police power alone. Meanwhile the *Shreve-port* doctrine took hold. This, together with the ex-panding area allowed for applying the local diversity branch of the *Cooley* formula, gave considerable room for escaping the trap. But economic change, with the increasing scope and variety of federal leg-islation which it induced, was forcing the trap shut.

Further details are not required. The short of the story is that the space from *Knight* to *Jones & Laughlin*, together with *Associated Press*[26] (1895-

---

[23] Northern Securities Co. v. United States, 193 U. S. 197.

[24] Standard Oil Co. v. United States, 221 U. S. 1; United States v. American Tobacco Co., 221 U. S. 106; United Mine Workers v Coronado Co., 259 U. S. 344; Coronado Co. v. United Mine Workers, 268 U. S. 295.

[25] See, for an application of this presumption to the exercise of power by Congress under the commerce clause, National Labor Re-lations Board v. Jones & Laughlin Steel Corp., 301 U. S. 1, 30-31.

[26] Associated Press v. National Labor Relations Board, 301 U. S. 103.

1937), represented a very wide swing in the federal affirmative pendulum from the states' rights-state power end of the arc to the national end. The pendulum did not swing steadily. It moved roughly, by jerks backward and forward. *Knight, Hammer v. Dagenhart, Adair v. United States,* and *Schechter Poultry* represent a direction, also a sequence of specific decision, hardly consistent with *Danbury Hatters, Standard Oil, American Tobacco, Coronado,* and other like decisions. The federal pendulum was swinging back and forth under the contrary pulls of the past and the future, driven by economic change and aversion to it, with the conflict between states' rights doctrine in the state power cases and the presumption that Congress too was acting constitutionally adding weight in opposite directions.

The pendulum finally came to rest with *Darby, Jones & Laughlin,* and *Associated Press.*[27] What has followed in their wake has been largely filling in and accommodation to their mandate. There still are limits to the federal commerce power, some placed by other constitutional limitations, such as due process,[28] not by the commerce clause itself; and other limits are dictated by considerations affecting the

---

[27] See the discussion in Wickard v. Filburn, 317 U. S. 111, 119 *et seq.*
[28] See North American Co. v. Securities & Exchange Commission, 327 U. S. 686, 705; United States v. Darby Lumber Co., 312 U. S. 100, 114-115; Gibbons v. Ogden, 9 Wheat. 1, 196.

43

necessary and appropriate scope for play of state rather than federal power. But the line marking those limits has been moved, perhaps in view of the early course of Marshall and others it is better to say moved back, a long way toward the federal end of the arc from where at one time it seemed to bid fair to stand. Who knows whether, if this had not been done, the nation could have gathered strength to meet the crises thrown up by the lawless state of international society in modern times? Who knows whether it could have preserved federal and democratic government against the crises of modern economic cycles?

II

The State Pendulum and the Implied Prohibition

THE commerce clause does not forbid the states to regulate commerce, in express terms. But its whole purpose was to break down the structure of interstate barriers the states were building. The clause would accomplish nothing if they could continue to act as they had been doing. By necessary negative inference, therefore, state power was limited to some extent. The clause was, as we have said, a two-edged blade. But the question really posed was the swath of the negatively cutting edge. By its very inferential character, the exclusion was lacking in precise definition of its scope. In this respect, several alternative inferences were permissible from the wording, as also concerning when and by whom the exclusion should be made. Those differences were substantial and in part irreconcilable. Hence the necessity and also the importance of choosing among them.

Processes of inference, especially of negative inference, are tricky. One need not be a logician to understand this. Particularly are they so when the choice is among multiple alternatives, logically possible, and these in turn govern choice among large and distinct courses of policy to be followed in governmental action.

The story is long and intricate, of the choice which has been made. It is composed of the stuff of history and policy, though these have been mixed with large measures of logic and fiction. Only the broader outlines can be traced.

Through it all is to be remembered that in the beginning, and on through the years, have been working the pulls of contrary doctrine and policies relating to emphasis, within the federal scheme, upon state as against national power. Here, as in other matters, the emphasis felt needed and proper by the judicial craftsman had place in his choice. "States' rights" pulled against "centralized government," which meant in this instance simply broad federal power.

Necessary also to recall is that at first it was not seen that large room for state action could be thought to coexist with broad congressional authority. Small wonder, in an age devoted to large generalizations and absolutes. Smaller still, when it is further remembered that not yet was it decided finally whether an enduring nation had been formed or only a loose league of states. Not without the largest influence upon the choices made, representing forward and backward swings of the pendulum, was the fact that the formative period in this body of our law lay in the time preceding and extending down to the Civil War.

With these things in mind, we turn to tracing the story of the earlier selections among the possible negative implications, which fixed the broader outlines of the law that has come out and survived.

At the outset it is just as well to state that, as the law has developed, the arc traveled by the negative pendulum has turned out not to be co-extensive with that in which the affirmative one oscillates. The scope of the prohibition against state action is not correlative, in any of the basic implications, with the full reach of the positive power given to Congress. But this was not always realized, particularly at the beginning. And this failure was to cause trouble. For Marshall's conception, not only of the breadth, but also of the "exclusiveness" of Congress' power, was to have profound influence upon the choice to be made, although it was due soon to be qualified.

Two other things already discussed also must be

47

kept in mind. First, as I have said, Marshall was bent primarily on establishing federal power and federal supremacy in the federal sphere; and his ideas of the scope of that sphere were not narrow. In the second place, he was dealing with the allocation of power; the states rather than the nation were the active agencies of regulation; the cases coming to him for decision involved primarily their action, not that of Congress;[1] and the extent of the prohibition had an obvious, though not defined, relationship to the scope of the federal power.

The time too was one for "spacious generalities" and Marshall loved them. They were effective tools for achieving his larger purposes and he made full use of their potentialities. Accordingly, in view of the way in which the questions came to him, he was defining the scope of Congress' power at the same time that he was determining the scope of the implied prohibition on the states. In other words he was defining the national power in a backhanded approach, though this was hardly a handicap to him.

Since the very basis of the excluding implication was that state power and the power given to Congress could not coexist completely, the conclu-

---

[1]But see Part 1, note 10, as to Gibbons v. Ogden, 9 Wheat. 1. The same is true of Brown v. Maryland, 12 Wheat. 419.

sion that they were mutually and totally exclusive, so that the two edges of the commerce instrument would be coextensive, was obviously available. It also fitted Marshall's broad purposes admirably. He was not hesitant to seize the opportunity. Hence he declared that whatever lay within the field given over to Congress was beyond the reach of any state action which properly could be regarded as "regulation."[2] Thus there could not be two "regulatory" powers operative in the some area at the same time.

This doctrine of total exclusiveness had profound effect in fixing the law of the prohibition. For by it the very existence of the congressional power, without reference to its having been exercised, outlawed state "regulation." But by this very fact also the doctrine was to run into head winds. Others were not so devoted to federal power broadly conceived and to federal supremacy. Their voices would be heard in time. A vast volume of state legislation which today is sustained would have to go out the window, if the great Virginian's idea of complete exclusiveness had come down unmodified. One has

---

[2] "But, when a State proceeds to regulate commerce with foreign nations, or among the several States, it is exercising the very power that is granted to Congress, and is doing the very thing which Congress is authorized to do." Gibbons v. Ogden, 9 Wheat. 1, 199-200. See IV Beveridge, The Life of John Marshall (1919) 434 ff.

only to think of this to realize that Marshall was reaching out for power, as he had done before; and in this instance, as in others, went farther than the case or the problem before him required. But this was part of his art.

The idea of complete "exclusiveness" was one of three elements in Marshall's conception of the commerce power, to each of which he gave broad sweep. Coupled with his broad definition of commerce and an equally broad idea of "regulation," the sweeping notion of "exclusiveness" made a trinitarian conception of the power which, had it remained unmodified, would have played havoc with the power of the states to protect vital interests of the people and of the commerce itself. Conceivably too it might have forced Congress into active regulation of business very much earlier than the time when, as things turned out, it undertook this course.

Moreover the broad "exclusive" conception was not required by any language of the commerce clause, by any compelled negative inference from it, or by necessity for controlling the basic evils the clause was designed to cure. Not all state regulation had given birth to those evils, but only that which specifically created them. Fully applied, the unmodified trinity would have gone far toward creating a centralized government, degrading the states, in a time when the conditions of living and working did not justify such consequences or require them in order to secure adequate controls; and when the general climate of governmental philosophy would not have tolerated them.

The trinity, as has been stated, aided Marshall in achieving his prime governmental objectives. Nevertheless, for the reasons given, some one of his broad elements had to give way. Time has confirmed Marshall's ideas in two of them. Thus, his broad conception of "commerce" has stood, though not without wavering, as we have shown. As to "regulation," the effects of powers when exercised, rather than their labels or purported abstract "nature," came to be the more important thing.[3] Not "regulation" therefore or "commerce," but "complete exclusion," was to give way. Not altogether, however. Exclusion the clause did provide. But it

---

[3] See Cooley v. Board of Wardens, 12 How. 299. But in many cases thereafter the term "a regulation of interstate commerce" was used as a "conclusion of law, and amounted to a statement of invalidity." Ribble, State and National Power over Commerce (1937) 107. In cases which sustained state statutes formulae such as the following were used: "It has been held that it is not every enactment which may incidentally affect commerce and the persons engaged in it that necessarily constitutes a regulation of commerce within the meaning of the Constitution." Western Union Telegraph Co. v. James, 162 U. S. 650, 656. "Nor is the statute of Kansas to be deemed a regulation of commerce among the States, simply because it may incidentally or indirectly affect such commerce." M-K-T Ry. v. Haber, 169 U. S. 613, 626-627.

was not necessarily or, as it turned out, appropriately, to be complete and total.

Taney cannot rightly be classified, for the greater portion of his career, as a zealous "states' righter." But in the 1850's he was an aging man, and the great shadow of the slavery issue with impending civil war was cast across the nation. His one gross decision on this question has concealed, for later generations, much of the true glory, it is not too much to say, of his earlier judicial work. His conception of the scope of Congress' power over commerce was not narrower than Marshall's.

But Taney was not given so much as Marshall to large generalization. He was an able, careful, and concrete jurist. If he went all the way with Marshall on the scope of Congress' power, he yet had a larger regard for the place of the states in the federal scheme. For him, it may be surprising to those who know him only as the author of an opinion in the *Dred Scott* case, the nation and the states were not essential antagonists, each seeking to exclude the other from power. He was rather a statesman of great common sense, except in the single instance, devoted to making workable accommodation between the two great powers in the federal scheme and giving appropriate place for each to act. Hence it was in reference to Marshall's idea of the exclusiveness of the federal power that Taney differed from his views. This difference related also to the part of judges in making the accommodation between nation and states. It gave rise to two great but essentially contrary currents which have flowed through the cases since it arose.

Before turning to them we should note that there is one area in which there is universal agreement, regardless of which conception of the implication is held in other respects. It comprehends the minimum possible exclusion under the clause, if it is to have exclusionary effect at all, as it must. It has never been disputed, in any view, that when Congress has legislated to regulate a matter falling within the field of the commerce which is interstate, its regulation nullifies any inconsistent local one. This all accept. But beyond this point, agreement stops. The disagreement begins therefore where Congress has not legislated[4] but has allowed its power to lie dormant. The grand enigma, in choosing the implication to be accepted, has been the "silence of Congress."

---

[4] Except for questions of interpretation bearing on the issue of consistency or inconsistency with state action. Cf. H. P. Welch Co. v. New Hampshire, 306 U. S. 79, 84: "Our decisions provide no formula for discovering implied effect of federal statutes upon state measures such as that under consideration."

The broad issue which it presents concerns the source, as well as the scope, of the prohibition. Shortly, does it arise and become applicable by virtue of the mere existence of power in Congress to regulate comerce, as Marshall declared, or must that power be exercised for the exclusion to come into play? Is the clause only a grant of power to Congress or is it also, in addition, a direct and immediately operative constitutional prohibition on state action? Numerous corollary questions and consequences follow from the answer which is made.

As has been said, the dormancy of Congress' power has generated two great but essentially contrary currents which originated from Taney's difference from Marshall.[5] Ultimately the difference concerns the respective functions of Court and of Congress in determining or applying the nullification of state action, as well as the breadth of the prohibition. But the opposing points of view more often are set forth in terms of immediate constitutional prohibition and, obversely, of prohibition effective only by intervening action of Congress, including

---

[5] "The categories of 'burdens' on interstate commerce, of state laws 'directly affecting' interstate commerce, etc., are natural concomitants of Marshall's doctrine. The theories as to the silence of Congress are the outgrowth of Taney's. When diverse theories cohabit, the miscegenation may produce strange progeny." Ribble, 204. See generally, in addition to Ribble's summary, Frankfurter, The Commerce Clause (1937); Biklé, The Silence of Congress (1927) 41 Harv. L. Rev. 200.

its "silence" as significant behavior.[6] By this latter notion hangs a long and interesting tale.

One view, flowing out of Marshall's emphasis upon the "exclusiveness" of Congress' power, has regarded the commerce clause as effective to nullify state laws "of its own force," without reference to any inference of Congress' intent from its silence. In this conception the Court becomes the instrument for executing a constitutional policy of implied negation dependent in no way upon congressional will. Almost from the day of its origin this view has been reiterated constantly in a line of cases extending down to the present time.[7]

The other idea matured through a long evolution from the quite different conceptions put forward by Taney.[8] As has been noted, his view parallels Marshall's philosophy concerning the breadth of Congress' power when affirmatively exercised. But it differs greatly in the negative phase. This difference lies in the fact that it attributes ultimate authority

---

[6] *Ibid.*

[7] Perhaps the most consistent exemplifications are represented in the lines of decision running from Welton v. Missouri, 91 U. S. 275, dealing with discriminatory state taxes, and headed by Wabash, St. L. & P. Ry. v. Illinois, 118 U. S. 557, relating to state regulation of interstate transportation. See Nippert v. Richmond, 327 U. S. 416, and authorities cited.

[8] See note 5. The culmination of this evolution came in Bowman v. Chicago & Northwestern Ry., 125 U. S. 465. See Ribble's discussion, at 72-85. But cf. Gavit, The Commerce Clause (1932) 7, 19.

55

to Congress, when silent just as when vocal, save only for the function of defining what is commerce and thus what is wholly outside the circle of Congress' authority. Implied negations of state power, like affirmative exertions of federal, come from Congress, not from the courts or from the Constitution operating independently of Congress' will. The silence of Congress, like its speech, is its own voice, effective to exclude any other. Whether that silence bespeaks consent or prohibition in a particular situation is mooted.[9] But in every case, under either inference, state law will stand or fall by the will of Congress, not by the independent will of the courts or immediate constitutional command.[10]

A third conception reduces the prohibition to the minimum possible one which has been stated above. It attributes no effect to Congress' silence either as forbidding or as supporting state action. But it regards the commerce clause as imposing no restriction whatever upon the states in the absence of positive action by Congress. Only when Congress legislates and does so inconsistently with the state's action is that action outlawed. This view has never been accepted by the Supreme Court. But from

---

[9]"The silence of Congress was accordingly ambiguous. It might mean prohibition or ratification of state laws." Ribble, 81; Gavit, The Commerce Clause (1932) 5, n. 6, 7 and text.

[10] Cf. note 7.

the very beginning it has had strong support from individual adherents,[11] subject to possible reservation concerning clearly discriminatory state action.[12] It is subject also, of course, to restrictions placed upon

---

[11] That the question was discussed but not settled in the Constitutional Convention itself, appears from debate on September 15, 1787, two days before submission of the proposed Constitution to Congress, a portion of which bears quotation:

"Mr. Mc.Henry & Mr. Carrol moved that 'no State shall be restrained from laying duties of tonnage for the purpose of clearing harbours and erecting light-houses'.

"Col. Mason in support of this explained and urged the situation of the Chesapeak which peculiarly required expences of this sort.

"Mr. Govr. Morris. The States are not restrained from laying tonnage as the Constitution now Stands. The exception proposed will imply the Contrary, and will put the States in a worse condition than the gentleman (Col. Mason) wishes.

"Mr. Madison. Whether the States are now restrained from laying tonnage duties depends on the extent of the power 'to regulate commerce'. These terms are vague but seem to exclude this power of the States— They may certainly be restrained by Treaty. He observed that there were other objects for tonnage Duties as the support of Seamen &c. He was more & more convinced that the regulation of Commerce was in its nature indivisible and ought to be wholly under one authority.

"Mr. Sherman. The power of the U. States to regulate trade being supreme can controul interferences of the State regulations (when) such interferences happen; so that there is no danger to be apprehended from a concurrent jurisdiction.

"Mr. Langdon insisted that the regulation of tonnage was an essential part of the regulation of trade, and that the States ought to have nothing to do with it. On motion 'that no State shall lay any duty on tonnage without the Consent of Congress'.

"N. H—ay— Mas. ay. Ct. divd. N. J. ay. Pa. no: Del. ay. Md. ay. Va. no. N-C. no. S-C. ay. Geo. no. [Ayes—6; noes—4; divided—1:]" II Farrand, Records of the Federal Constitutional Convention of 1787 (1911) 625-626.

See Note, Congressional Consent to Discriminatory State Legislation (1945) 45 Col. L. Rev. 927, 946 ff., for a short summary of views expressed in the debates and later by members of the Convention. See also Abel, The Commerce Clause in the Constitutional Convention and in Contemporary Comment (1941) 25 Minn. L. Rev. 432.

[12] E. g., " , . . state laws are not invalid under the Commerce Clause

57

the powers of both Congress and the states by other constitutional limitations and upon Congress' authority by the outer limits of the commerce power itself.

The first two conceptions have embodied acceptance or accommodation of Curtis' master distinction in *Cooley* v. *Board of Wardens* between matters requiring uniformity of regulation and matters sufficiently local to permit variety.[13] Under the one thesis the *Cooley* distinction is taken as a criterion of state power imposed directly by the Constitution. Under the other it works as a formula for determining the meaning of Congress' silent will.[14] The third conception, logically, would reject the distinction entirely.[15]

---

unless they actually discriminate against interstate commerce or conflict with a regulation enacted by Congress." Gwin, White & Prince v. Henneford, 305 U. S. 434, dissenting opinion at 446.

" . . . except for state acts designed to impose discriminatory burdens on interstate commerce because it *is* interstate—Congress alone must 'determine how far [interstate commerce] . . . shall be free and untrammeled, how far it shall be burdened by duties and imposts, and how far it shall be prohibited.' " *Id.* at 455.

See also, for essentially the same position, Adams Mfg. Co. v. Storen, 304 U. S. 307, dissenting opinion; McCarroll v. Dixie Greyhound Lines, Inc., 309 U. S. 176, dissenting opinion; Southern Pacific Co. v. Arizona, 325 U. S. 761, dissenting opinion at 795.

[13] Cooley v. Board of Wardens, 12 How. 299, 319.

[14] See Ribble, State and National Power over Commerce 72-85.

[15] With the possible exception for clearly discriminatory state laws. See note 12. The apparent inconsistency of the idea that discriminatory state taxes may be invalid, even in the absence of action by Congress, with the other idea that the commerce clause lays no prohibition

Strange is it that time has not put the basic controversy wholly to rest. Each of the first two views has been dominant at different periods, but neither ever exclusively since the second matured. Each has persisted, often in unqualified assertion without reference to the concurrent operation of the other.[16] More often the two have been lumped in confused admixture, unintended or deliberate.[17] But by one means or another escape from irrevocable clash always has been found.

Several avenues have opened. Confusion aside, the shifting of emphasis from dogma and formulae

---

upon state action "of its own force" (see text at note 7) is more apparent than real, if discrimination in this sense is limited to those taxes or regulations which actually or inherently produce the two effects specified in Bethlehem Motors Co. v. Flynt, 256 U. S. 421, 427. In that case the opinion stated, "It is the finding of the court that the automobiles were in the hands of the agents of the consigning corporations, and therefore, a tax against them was practically a tax on their importation into the State. It is not necessary to say it would be useless to send them to the State if their sale could be prevented *by a prohibitive tax or one so discriminating that it would prevent competition with the products of the State.*" (Emphasis added.) For, so limited, the prohibitive effect of the commerce clause, absent action by Congress, would be substantially a translation to interstate commerce of the policy of the express prohibitions laid upon the states against laying imposts or duties on imports or exports, without the consent of Congress, by Article 1, §10; and against laying any duty of tonnage, also without Congress' consent, by the same clause.

[16] Cf. notes 7 and 8 and text.

[17] See Ribble, 202-203. "The confusion will appear in the language of the Court when, forgetting or ignoring the expressions of exclusiveness, it declares for a concurrent power . . . Though the Court has not been happy in the expression of these doctrines, it has been wise in that the doctrines developed leave to it great freedom of decision." Ribble, 203, 211.

to practical effects in commerce law problems has played a very large part.[18] Equally important perhaps are two other factors. For one, cases did not arise with facts so shaped as quite to compel the ultimate choice. The other and principal escape was through the almost boundless scope which the undefined negation gave to judges for filling the void of the implied constitutional prohibition or, alternatively, of Congress' silent will.

This liberty was as great for the one as for the other conception. Rare indeed will be the case in which the same prohibition or freedom for state action cannot be found in the silence of Congress, whether as an inference of its will or as a conclusion from the effect of the commerce clause operating independently of that will. To consider a state law as consistent with Congress' will, expressed by its silence, is almost to concede its constitutionality;[19] and, conversely, to conceive the Constitution as forbidding specific state action is tantamount to re-

[18] See note 17. See also Nippert v. Richmond, 327 U. S. 416; Best & Co. v. Maxwell, 311 U. S. 454; cf. Prudential Ins. Co. v. Benjamin, 328 U. S. 408. See also Wechsler, Stone and the Constitution (1946) 46 Col. L. Rev. 764, 785-787.

[19] Cf. note 20. For the Cooley v. Board of Wardens rule, put in terms of "silence of Congress," see, e.g., Transportation Co. v. Parkersburg, 107 U. S. 691, 701-704. See also the dissenting opinion in Morgan v. Virginia, 328 U. S. 373, at 394.

garding Congress' silently expressed will as not tolerating that action.[20]

In theory the two grounds are vastly different. But, practically speaking, for purposes of initial decision at least, the difference is largely verbal.[21] In no instance has Congress' silent action been held unconstitutional. It is hardly possible for such an instance to occur. Judges unfettered by positive wording of the Constitution and free also, through Congress' silence, to find its intent, are not apt to discover this in ideas which would contravene their constitutional conceptions, thus filling the void only to turn and empty it.

To take account of these practical workings of the judicial mind does not mean necessarily that the idea of action by Congress through remaining silent is altogether imaginary or delusive, having no connection whatever with reality or validity in experience. True, as an original matter, it would seem highly dubious to treat anything as legislation

---

[20] The latter conclusion, of course, follows automatically; and the former almost so. In fact, whether or not the two questions are formally put as separate and distinct issues, each arises ordinarily in such a situation that thinking about it hardly can be separated from influence of the other exerted subconsciously, if not in explicit rationalization.

[21] That is, for any specific issue of this sort not previously decided it is practically as easy to reach one conclusion as another, whether grounding is found in the one theory or the other. But this possibility takes on vital importance for later cases where intervening action by Congress has taken place to repudiate, in effect, what the Court has decided. See authorities cited in notes 23 and 24.

other than bills duly enacted according to constitutionally prescribed procedures. But, aside from that factor, institutions like individuals, Congress among them, may give expression to group attitudes, may indeed act, by maintaining silence in circumstances which give it meaning.[22]

Nevertheless this form of expression has great dangers when taken as equivalent to legislation. Apart from disregarding constitutionally imposed procedures for enacting legislation, it lends itself readily to inference of what the observer wishes to find. Judges are not immune to this tendency. In rare instances intended meaning will be plain. More often alternative or multiple possibilities, perhaps equally tenable, will be offered. And nearly always is present the strong chance that the silence may be meaningful of nothing more than sheer neutrality, of intent to express no purpose or attitude whatsoever. Finally this process of inference lacks the usual supporting evidences of Congress' specific intent which the normal and formal functioning of the legislative process affords.

In sum, for determining the effects of the com-

---

[22] The basis is not merely legal, as reflected in the many cases which have found significance in Congress' silence, whether accurately to accord with its actual intent or otherwise; it is also psychological. See, e.g., McDougall, The Group Mind (1920). See also Cleveland v. United States, 329 U. S. 14, concurring opinion at 21.

merce clause upon state legislation, inference from the silence of Congress assumed to be meaningful added its own peculiar dangers for confusion and misconception to those generally inherent in a process of implied negation on the level of constitutional command.

Those pitfalls have been most obvious perhaps in the situations where the silence of Congress or the dormancy of its power has been taken judicially, on one view or the other of its constitutional effects, to forbid state action, only to have Congress later disclaim the prohibition or undertake to nullify it.[23] Not yet has the Supreme Court held such a disclaimer invalid or that state action supported by it could not stand. On the contrary, in each instance the Court has given effect to the congressional judgment contradicting its own previous one.[24]

This cannot be taken with any assurance as having involved only a change of heart concerning what

---

[23] See Prudential Ins. Co. v. Benjamin, 328 U. S. 408, 424, and n. 28; see also Ribble, c. X; Biklé, The Silence of Congress (1927) 41 Harv. L. Rev. 200; Powell, Validity of State Legislation under the Webb-Kenyon Act (1917) 2 So. L. Q. 112; Dowling, Interstate Commerce and State Power (1940) 27 Va. L. Rev. 1; Congressional Consent to Discriminatory State Legislation (1945) 45 Col. L. Rev. 927.

[24] Pennsylvania v. Wheeling and Belmont Bridge Co., 13 How. 518, with which compare Pennsylvania v. Wheeling and Belmont Bridge Co., 18 How. 421, and The Clinton Bridge, 10 Wall. 454; Leisy v. Hardin, 135 U. S. 100, with which compare In re Rahrer, 140 U. S. 545; Bowman v. Chicago & Northwestern Ry., 125 U. S. 465, with which compare Clark Distilling Co. v. Western Maryland Ry., 242 U. S. 311, Cf. Prudential Ins. Co. v. Benjamin, 328 U. S. 408.

was Congress' will. For while the reversed decisions purported to find its will in Congress' silence, the opinions also give basis for believing that reliance may have been placed at the same time upon the immediately operative effect of the commerce clause[25] and the dissenting opinion of Mr. Justice McLean in the second *Wheeling Bridge* case, 18 How. 421, 437, strengthens this view. Thereby, to whatever extent the commerce clause was considered immediately effective, another enigma has been created. If the commerce clause itself forbids state action "by its own force," how is it that Congress by expressly consenting can give that action validity?

The apparent dilemma does not arise under either variant of the view that the commerce clause lays no restraint on state power "of its own force." But it has caused trouble under the contrary and prevailing view. I shall not undertake to elucidate the reconciliations which have been attempted.[26] The fact is, of course, that Congress in these cases was not lifting itself by its bootstraps.

---

[25] In addition to the opinions, which thus represent the tendency to avoid square choice between the opposing theories, cf. text beginning at note 5, see Ribble's discussion in State and National Power over Commerce (1937) 62, 206-214. See also Prudential Ins. Co. v. Benjamin, 328 U.S. 408, n. 33.

[26] See the authorities cited in note 23. The Supreme Court has not been concerned in its opinions with the theoretical difficulties. See Southern Pacific Co. v. Arizona, 325 U. S. 761, 769-770; Prudential Ins. Co. v. Benjamin, 328 U. S. 408, 424-427.

The dilemma was only apparent, not real. It was the product of arguments, and of opinions rendered, in the early leading cases dealing explicitly with the power of Congress and the states, acting conjointly, to regulate navigation, the so-called *Wheeling Bridge* cases. It arose from the idea that the dormancy of Congress' power was equivalent to prohibition of state action by express legislation and then, by a curious twist, from adding the conception that the state exclusion was as broad as the grant of power to Congress. Since, further, the state prohibition was derived from the Constitution, Congress itself could not surmount it and by express enactment authorize the states to do an "unconstitutional" thing. Thus, by the idea of equivalence between congressional power and state prohibition was the commerce clause itself inverted into a limitation on Congress' power to regulate commerce, an idea manifestly absurd.[27] But this was not all. For the effect was to make the clause also a restriction upon the combined powers of Congress and the states acting conjointly and consistently. It was, in other words, to outlaw all power in the federal system. The "silence of Congress"

[27] But see the dissenting opinion of Mr. Justice McLean in the second *Wheeling Bridge* case, 18 How. at 442.

has not attained greater stature at any time than in the opinions reflecting this conception and consequence.

There is of course no such equivalence between the scope of the federal power and that of the implied prohibition upon the states. Nor is the dormancy of Congress' power equivalent to its fullest possible exertion by formal legislative enactment, either to sustain or to forbid state action. Fortunately those assumptions have never received lasting support. They are now expressly repudiated.[28] But their acceptance by able lawyers and judges shows how far the processes of assumption and inference may carry one, whether made from the amorphous implied negative of the commerce clause or from the vacuum of Congress' silence considered as having positive legislative effect.

Time and decision have given validity to the view that the commerce clause "of its own force" does prohibit state regulation. They also have confirmed that there is imbalance, nonequivalence in

---

[28] See Prudential Ins. Co. v. Benjamin, 328 U. S. 408, 421. In each of the cases outlawing state taxes found to discriminate against interstate commerce, "the question of validity of the state taxing statute arose when Congress' power lay dormant. In none had Congress acted or purported to act, either by way of consenting to the state's tax or otherwise. Those cases therefore presented no question of the validity of such a tax where Congress had taken affirmative action consenting to it or purporting to give it validity. Nor, consequently, could they stand as controlling precedents for such a case."

the length of its affirmatively and its negatively cutting edges. But from *Cooley v. Board of Wardens* to now the question of how much difference has been litigated.

That great decision gave a rubric in the test of uniformity. But this too has left large room for expanding and contracting the arc through which the nullifying pendulum swings. Apart from the confusion created by imputing legislative effects to Congress' silence, which was no part of the *Cooley* distinction but was only glossed on it by some, judges do not automatically agree upon what requires uniformity and what does not. Here too considerations of policy have swayed their judgments.

In the long flood of litigation which the prohibitive aspect of the commerce clause has created, Marshall's universal exclusion has been rejected; and Taney's denial of any implied direct constitutional exclusion, in his transfer of the exclusion from constitutional grounding to legislative foundation in Congress' silence, likewise has not stood the test of time.

But the gist of Marshall's work has survived. And Taney's work aided in bringing it down to practical proportions appropriate for a federal democracy, in which the states and the Congress largely may work together, concurrently regulating commerce, but in which still the federal power is supreme, will override inconsistent local action, and on occasion will enable the states to act where otherwise they might not do so.[29]

The negative pendulum, like the positive one, has swung back and forth between the state and the national poles of power. Again I shall not attempt to trace detail. At times, especially when the federal commerce power was by way of being contracted, the prohibitive arc was lengthening. The sum of the two effects, where they conjoined, was to outlaw the possibility of regulation in broad areas of commerce. But, just as in recent years the permissible scope for congressional commerce action has broadened, returning to Marshall's conception, the prohibitive effect of the clause has been progressively narrowed. The trend has been toward sustaining state regulation formerly regarded as inconsistent with Congress' unexercised power over commerce. To the extent this has occurred, the positive and negative pendulums have moved more and more in unison, not as mutually exclusive but as more mutually tolerant.

Nevertheless, the general problem of adjustment

---

[29] See Prudential Ins. Co. v. Benjamin, 328 U. S. 408, and other cases cited in note 24 supra.

remains. It has only been transferred to a level more tolerant of both state and federal legislative action. On this level a new or renewed emphasis on facts and practical considerations has been allowed to work. Notwithstanding this, old doctrine retains influence. Dogma and formulae, reflecting the certitude of earlier swings in policy, continue to appear. Practical considerations and outworn theories at times remain commingled, so as to obscure, if not quite conceal, underlying conflicts of theory and policy concerning the negation's proper scope and application. This resulting pattern, if not kaleidoscopic, still affords highly convenient variables for decision in specific controversies.[30] More often than might be expected from such a footing, reconcilable results have been secured. But rationalization which straddles conflict or ignores it leads eventually to irreconcilable results and thus to necessity for reformulating reasoning.

This has been the broad history of the commerce clause. The judicial task continues. Troublesome questions still arise, and frequently. But the scope of judicial intervention has been narrowed by the more recent trends, affecting both the affirmative and the prohibitive workings of the

---

[30] See the decisions cited in Prudential Ins. Co. v. Benjamin, 328 U. S. 408, 420, n. 18.

clause. Greater leeway and deference are given for legislative judgments, national and state, formally expressed. Larger emphasis is put on scrutiny of particular facts and concrete consequences, with an eye on their practical bearing for creating the evils the commerce clause was designed to outlaw. Correspondingly, less stress, though in my opinion still too much, is placed upon large generalizations and dogmatisms inherited from levels of debate time has lowered. More and more the controlling considerations of policy implicit in thinking, judgment, and decision are brought into the open.

Some sources of vast confusion have been cleared out. The early broad idea of complete and total mutual "exclusiveness" departed with *Cooley v. Board of Wardens*, never to return. The "silence of Congress," taken as an expression of legislative will, no longer is adequate for outlawing state laws.[31] Judges do not now seem to find conflict between what the state has done and what Congress has not done in its "silently expressed will." Like others, judicial fingers burnt tend to avoid the flame. The idea that Congress has "occupied the field," and thereby precluded legislation by the

---

[31] The most that can be said is that in some situations the idea of finding consent or prohibition in Congress' silence furnishes a tenable basis for disposing of the particular problem and in some others a convenient if not altogether tenable escape from theoretical difficulty.

states, though not altogether eliminated, works within narrower confines. The search here is properly for irreconcilable inconsistency, with emphasis upon reconciliation wherever possible, in the place of earlier easy finding of occupancy. Real and inescapable conflict there must be, absent express congressional preëmption, when the basis for outlawing state action is conflict with Congress' declared policies within its field of primacy. More and more, too, Congress and the states have come to work harmoniously, dovetailing their legislation in the regulation of commerce. And the notion has been put to rest, one may hope, that the commerce clause is itself either a limitation upon Congress' power within the field of commerce or one upon the conjoined and consistent exercise of the powers of Congress and the states. Finally, some sad experiences with judicial conceptions of the need for uniformity[32] have made judges unwilling to jump too readily to the conclusion that this branch of the Cooley formula applies.[33]

Nevertheless the dormancy of Congress' power

---

[32] See Part I, note 13.
[33] Cf., e. g., South Carolina State Highway Dept. v. Barnwell Bros., 303 U. S. 177; Western Live Stock v. Bureau of Revenue, 303 U. S. 250; McGoldrick v. Berwind-White Co., 309 U. S. 33; Nelson v. Sears, Roebuck & Co., 312 U. S. 359; California v. Thompson, 313 U. S. 109; Duckworth v. Arkansas, 314 U. S. 390; Union Brokerage Co. v. Jensen, 322 U. S. 202; Robertson v. California, 328 U. S. 440.

still gives occasion, within these more restricted lines, for the implied prohibition of the commerce clause to work. The exclusion, narrowing with the years, has come on the whole to require substantial danger, real or actually threatening, of creating the effects the clause was drawn to prevent. If this is not invariable, it is unquestionably the more general trend. In this restricted area the debate still goes on. It will continue. For here room remains for continuing difference in policy and in judgment of effects. In some part this is unavoidable, as is true in application of other constitutional provisions.

But to say this is merely to say that the Constitution was built for the ages. One reason for its enduring quality has been that it made room for the continuing adjustment and readjustment of federal-state relationships, without which no federal scheme could long survive. So vast and complex a mechanism cannot be inflexibly rigid in the interworking of such vital and coördinate parts.

The commerce clause has been by no means perfect in its application and administration. Some large blunders there have been; others no doubt will be. But on the whole the clause has accomplished its great objective. From the disunited states of 1786, which interstate trade barriers had created, has grown the United States of 1946. No small part of that growth has been due to the effects of the commerce clause and its administration. Perhaps no other constitutional provision has played a greater part.

That part must continue if the nation would remain great and democratic. A balkanized America today would be vulnerable to attack from without and would be unequal to maintaining our people within. Our dream comprehends something more than a subsistence level of living. For tomorrow as for yesterday, it can be realized only by giving the commerce clause its originally intended application.

III

Observations for Federal Democratic Living

IN THESE lectures I have declared my faith in the universality of the legal principle, which today offers the only alternative to the rule of unbridled physical power. On this choice depends whether the force men have created will destroy the civilization they have worked so long to build or, on the other hand, put to such use alone, that force will perpetuate and infinitely expand our civilization. Upon this issue, until the event proves otherwise beyond all hope or peradventure, no man and no nation can afford to surrender faith, faith in the legal principle and in its eventual universal application and establishment. Any other course would be suicidal.

I have stated my belief also in the federal principle, rooted in our own experience. It has made this nation great and at the same time has kept the country democratic. Not perfection of greatness or of democracy, but a continuing process of perfecting both, has been achieved. In this the commerce clause has had a powerful, if administratively intricate, part.

We have seen how a federal plan has worked, against the greatest obstacles for sixteen decades, toward creating liberty and justice under law. And I have tried to show, inadequately, how it has operated in one of the most complex problems of a federal state, imperfectly and with almost constant oscillation of powers, but nevertheless on the whole to accomplish the allocations of authority, made essential by its diversification in such a scheme, to the satisfaction of our people.

A federal system is not created in a day, a year, or even a decade. Our fathers did not construct the framework of our own until more than a decade after they declared our independence and more than half that time after they had won it finally. We cannot be less patient today than they were in their time. For we have altogether as much at stake. Their work now depends on what we do. It may be that the federal principle, with time, will afford the solution for the world's dilemma now impending. We of all people, by force of our experience, should be the last to deny its virtue or efficacy.

It may seem strange to think of a purely commercial power as one of the foundations of democratic institutions. But in my judgment this is just what the commerce clause has turned out to be. It is inherently a federal device. And such a plan, by its very division of powers, creates a safeguard perhaps not otherwise attainable against wholly autocratic action. A democratic nation must have a government endowed with powers sufficient to meet its external and internal needs. These today necessarily must be large. But there is safety now, as there was when our fathers acted and *The Federalist* was being written, in distributing those powers so that they may not be concentrated altogether in one place.

The commerce clause, short as it is, has worked to this end admirably. The Congress, the state, and the courts have all had important and continuing parts in the regulation of the nation's commerce. They will keep on doing so. That power, so distributed, has been a major protection to individual freedom from concentrated authority in any single place over the lifeblood of the people, their commerce and trade. At the same time, by outlawing the balkanizing power of the states, it has given them the legal and economic foundations which have released their native energies and abilities for the country's vast and rapid development. If a floor of economic security and freedom is essential to maintaining the other great freedoms of mind and heart with all that goes to make up our prized individual liberty, the essence of democracy, the commerce clause has had part also in this.

Further observations would be superfluous. The commerce clause has done its great and essential work in creating our federal democracy. I have hope and faith that similar blessings may be perpetuated for ourselves and our children for an indefinite future. I have grave doubt that, in the conditions of our time, they can be perpetuated for us unless they are established and maintained for men everywhere. The federal principle, applied to create liberty under law, is the basic tool by which our people have attained this goal. I believe that it may be used for satisfying the universal need now so apparent. May we and others have the vision, the will, and the courage of the founding fathers to do this.

Cases Cited

Below are listed the cases referred to in the text and cited in footnotes on the pages indicated. So that the cases themselves may be more readily accessible, references are given also to legal sources not mentioned in the footnotes.

	PAGE
Adams Mfg. Co. v. Storen, 304 U.S. 307 58 S. Ct. 913, 82 L. Ed. 1365 (1939)	58
Alabama v. King & Boozer, 314 U.S. 1 62 S. Ct. 43, 86 L. Ed. 3 (1941)	35
Associated Press v. National Labor Relations Board, 301 U.S. 103 57 S. Ct. 650, 81 L. Ed. 392 (1936)	42
Best & Co. v. Maxwell, 311 U.S. 454 61 S. Ct. 334, 85 L. Ed. 275 (1940)	60
Bethlehem Motors Co. v. Flynt, 256 U.S. 421, 427 41 S. Ct. 571, 65 L. Ed. 1029 (1920)	59
Board of Education v. Barnette, 319 U.S. 624 63 S. Ct. 1178, 87 L. Ed. 1628 (1942)	25
Bowman v. Chicago & Northwestern Ry., 125 U.S. 465 8 S. Ct. 689, 31 L. Ed. 700 (1887)	55, 63
Brown v. Maryland, 12 Wheat. 419 6 L. Ed. 678 (1827)	48
California v. Thompson, 313 U.S. 109 61 S. Ct. 930, 85 L. Ed. 1219 (1940)	71
Cantwell v. Connecticut, 310 U.S. 296 60 S. Ct. 900, 84 L. Ed. 1213 (1939)	25
Clark Distilling Co. v. Western Maryland Ry., 242 U.S. 311 37 S. Ct. 180, 61 L. Ed. 326 (1916)	63
Cleveland v. United States, 329 U.S. 14 67 S. Ct. 361, 91 L. Ed. 1 (1946)	62
Clinton Bridge, The, 10 Wall. 454 19 L. Ed. 969 (1870)	31, 63
Cooley v. Board of Wardens, 12 How. 299, 319 13 L. Ed. 997 (1851)	37, 51, 58, 60, 67, 70
Coronado Co. v. United Mine Workers, 268 U.S. 295 45 S. Ct. 514, 69 L. Ed. 963 (1924)	42

79

CASES CITED